B4 Earth We Were Here

GREGORY GORDON JR.

authorHOUSE

AuthorHouse™
1663 Liberty Drive
Bloomington, IN 47403
www.authorhouse.com
Phone: 1 (800) 839-8640

Published by AuthorHouse 06/30/2020

ISBN: 978-1-7283-6593-0 (sc)
ISBN: 978-1-7283-6592-3 (e)

Print information available on the last page.

This book is printed on acid-free paper.

Chapter 1

I am successful… I am rich in spirit… God handles my battles… I'm learning to turn away from all of my evil ways… God the Father is good to me…He forgives me even when I know I'm wrong. He teaches me and guides me through the day…I don't sleep anymore I have visions when I close my eyes, God takes me on trips around the universe…Last night God placed me on top of the moon, I was the brightest star in the universe, I took a ride on the moon around the universe, I didn't see anything but space… and Angels looking at me as if they were confused, but this one particular angel approached me, and kept disappearing as if she was checking on me… keeping an eye on me… I didn't know why the angel kept popping up checking on me but every time she popped up… I felt a rush of energy, an amazing feeling, the feeling of a child receiving Christmas presents on Christmas Day… I was over excited, God waited until I was sound asleep to take my soul on what I would call a field trip, space trip… See THIS WAS JUST THE BEGINNING B4 Earth we were here…

Chapter 2

Before Earth we were here, I can remember when my insight first started, the first time I recognized My Spiritual Father was speaking to me... I was 3 years old. It was the month of December...year 1988.

My Dad had family day at his job he was a bellman at the Sheraton plaza in down town Chicago, I remember he woke me up early on a Saturday morning and said he was taking me to the North Pole and I was going to meet Santa, man the look on my face was priceless, he took me down there to his job, and there were hundreds of kids in line to meet Santa, and Santa said, "I'm going to randomly select a kid out of the crowd that is very blessed and chosen." And his helper, Mrs. Elf, repeated, "Blessed and Chosen!" and Santa said, "Yes, the special one" and he said who wants to be picked? I was standing to the far left towards the front and he said you with the cool Christmas sweater come here... I remember being real shy almost embarrassed because all eyes were on me, my dad said go up there and sit on Santa's knee, and he asked me what I wanted for Christmas and I told him a drum set, a microphone and a gold chain... all the parents and kids started laughing and as Santa kept asking me questions I realized the other children liked me and where amazed that I got picked I remember going home happy with a smile on my face from ear to ear, I jumped in my mom arms and told her the good news and she rewarded me as usual for doing something good, that use to motivate me to be even more positive towards people in life, before I knew anything about the cruel world today, I was a happy loving angel, after a week passing, I remember coming home from school and my pops threw me a newspaper and said look son in it was a picture of me getting interviewed on Santa's lap talking to a crowd of kids with huge smiles on their face telling the media They wish they was that kid, and that kid was me... I knew then I was destined. I knew I was different, this was the beginning after the beginning but before it got to this point allow me to introduce how we even got into this shell that we call flesh, this ball we call Earth, this form we call life, before Earth we were here...

Chapter 3

I remember standing next to the creator, in the heavens outside of the universe, with trillions and trillions of stars, angels what we call them mingling not having a clue what sin is, innocent, and pure... I remember there was this one star that shined brighter than any other star outside of the galaxy... her name was Lucy, Lucy was beyond beautiful and had the most soulful voice you could ever hear... Lucy was very charming, but her voice was made of gold, Lucy voice was so beautiful when she sang the whole entire universe got quiet, and felt a blast of good energy run thru there conscious, but unconscious soul... Lucy voice was so amazing even The creator was amazed at the way Lucy used the gift he gave her... the creator found Lucy not only more alert than the other stars, but he seen the best in her, because Lucy voice was so great the creator rewarded her with a position of power, he granted Lucy with her own room, a room of life... every star outside of the galaxy loved Lucy... whenever Lucy felt she needed a break away from all of the attention Lucy would go to her room, her own little world of life... where she had full control of... one day The creator told Lucy he needed to charge, rest what we call it here on Earth, As the creator was resting, Lucy decided to invite certain stars to her room, as she was inviting certain stars to her room some where going back telling the others about this magnificent room of Lucy's, all of the stars that got the message started to get excited about going to Lucy's magnificent room, Lucy realized that her room was very special and had a lot of attention on it, Lucy began to tell certain stars that they can't enter, trillions of stars were confused but still happy and humble… one moment Lucy decided to charge herself she started to realize every time she charge herself she becomes brighter… with a little more understanding than she did before, as Lucy was charging the creator awoke, he noticed the down faces the confused behavior, he asked one of his stars to come forth, this star name was Michael, he asked Michael why the down behavior, he replied there's no hope in entering Lucy's magnificent world. The creator smiled and said Michael do you want to enter into that room? Michael replied slowly, with a down look on his face… I want my own magnificent room, I want to shine brighter than any star outside of the universe… and the creator responded and said open your mouth, lift every voice and sing Michael like never before. Michael turned and opened his mouth and began to sing from the bottom of his soul, before you knew it everyone outside of the universe was at a standstill of amazement, even the creator found Michael beyond interesting, the creator was amazed with the way Michael used the gift he had gave him… Michael was very charming with a smile that pleased your soul as if you were looking at an innocent baby, and listening to the voice of your favorite R&B singer. At this point all attention got drew towards Michael, Lucy became confused it was a feeling that she had never experienced, a feeling of feeling down, Lucy decided to bring her special certain stars to her world and continued to deny other stars access to her room allowing them to experience a down feeling to the soul, The creator looked at Michael and asked him how would you like to visit Lucy's world, Michael replied with a shy smile and said that would be awesome, Lucy began to start throwing a temper tantrum and denied access to every star outside of the galaxy, the creator figured if she had enough alone time hiding in her room she would eventually come back out with a good spiritual consciousness feeling, but instead Lucy came up with another plan, she started to sing and manipulate the stars with her beautiful amazing voice and her bright charming gold looks... even at this point the creator was still amazed at the beautiful talent he introduced to Lucy, the beautiful gift of music that he gave to her...She called for all of her chosen stars to come to her room with her, with the permission of the creator. The creator gave her as she will, the desires that little Lucy wanted to fulfill. As time went on the creator started to notice strange behavior coming from the stars that were allowed to travel to Little Lucy's room, he started to notice that they were getting stronger thru the teachings of the position the creator handed to Lucy, at this point Lucy started to feel powerful she felt that because she was given the power to quiet the universe with her voice and looks, that the stars were in her favor and she can tell them anything and they would submit to her beautiful voice and charming gold look, at this point Lucy felt she was on top and in control of every existing star ever created outside and inside of the universe. At this point the creator allowed Lucy to feel that she was on top of the world he basically handed her over the key to his world even after knowing that Lucy was being manipulative, and making certain stars feel down and not as important as the creator made them feel...

Chapter 4

Lucy came to the creator and asked him if he needed some rest, if so she would make sure everything was decent and in order, the creator was at a standstill he immediately told Lucy that would be nice, where we were before Earth the creator didn't have to go into details about certain things, in the spiritual world what was done didn't need to be explained. The stars were pleased, the creator had allowed Lucy to bring certain stars into her room who she wanted there and those she didn't want there to give them their own section outside of the universe, time went by 3 days and 4 nights of rest (Earth time) the creator came back and was pleased Lucy had did exactly what he instructed her to do, he called Lucy and Michael to the front and had them lift there voice and sing to celebrate for a good thing had been done. The creator began to ask is there any star that wants to sing if so may the brightest star outside of the universe show itself. This one star came forth with a magnificent gold glow, but did not sing, the star just stood there and shined, the star shined so bright that it didn't have to open its voice to quiet the universe, the creator named this star Gabrielle, Gabrielle was beyond charming with a very strong demeanor of love a quietness of loyalty, to the creator, Lucy started to notice the attention the creator was giving to Michael and Gabrielle, she started to notice the other stars showing them attention as well, so Lucy felt she was losing friends at this point

Lucy became a downer spirit, Lucy stood up outside of the universe and opened her voice and said how would you like to come and live in my room with me, I will teach you how to become a pro creator, a third of the outside universe which would be about 75% of people on Earth of the outside universe agreed to that, at this point after the creator asked Lucy and Michael to come forth the creator hadn't spoke in 4 days as a third of the outside universe proceeded to follow Lucy, the creator said how would you all like to go live inside of Lucy's room? 88% of the stars decided that they wanted to come to Lucy's room and experience it. the other 12% that did not want to go to her room the creator gave them high positions outside of the galaxy, the power of 12 Lucy's in one, these stars did not have free will they had to go, do, and say whatever it was the creator wanted them to do.

power of 12 Lucy's in one, these stars did not have free will they had to go, do, and say whatever it was the creator wanted them to do.

Chapter 5

Lucy was starting to become agitated at the fact the creator wasn't giving her all of his attention anymore, almost as if he was fading away from her, she came to the creator and said this is my room why do you invite these starlets into my room, the creator responded I am not a creator of separation but the galaxy of love and the author of creation... you were once a starlet before you became a high ranked star, must you not forget where you come from, Lucy looked at the creator looking sad with the first feeling of being condemned, Lucy felt bad for the first time a confusing feeling she couldn't understand, at this point Lucy downer spirit was turning into hatred, and envy, because she couldn't understand the feeling or the behavior of the creator, the creator looked at Lucy and chuckled and calmly told her I love you Lucy with every piece of me that I used to create me. Lucy didn't know how to handle the confusing situation, so she began to rebel An flee from the things that were not in her favor, she started to become miserable and throw temper tantrums, and ball up and stay to herself, whenever she got bored and felt she needed company she would come back from her room and manipulate the outside universe with her voice and beautiful gold looks... even the creator would still be amazed at the creative way Lucy played with the gift he gave her, Lucy came to the creator and said with a down sad puppy face look and told the creator that she only wanted her room to herself, the creator granted Lucy her desires and gave her as she will.

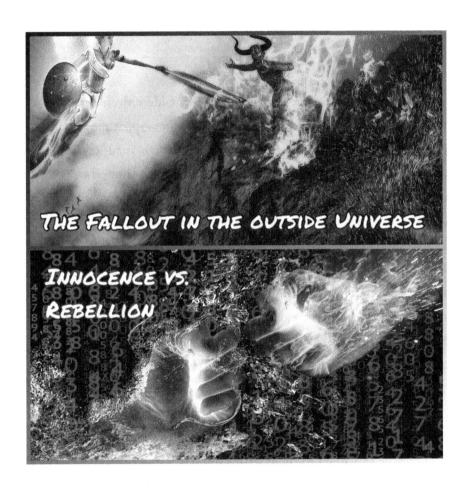

The Fallout in the outside Universe

Innocence vs. Rebellion

Chapter 6

The creator called for the attention of the outside universe, as he had every stars undivided conscious but non conscious spirit present in his presence. He pulled up a design of a model of a human made in the image of a star, he explained to the stars what this was, he showed us images of people living in houses, driving cars, eating, drinking, flying in planes just as clear as if you were staring me in the eyes... face to face, he showed us water he showed us fire, he showed us life... the entire outside galaxy were beyond over excited, a feeling so good you can't even imagine, the spiritual body we were in b4 we came to Earth was even more beautiful than flesh... the bottom half of our body waist down was made of a blueish gold fire the blue as if you was to light a stove when it first cuts on... the upper body was made of pure gold that was transparent, the legs, and feet was made of fire every starlet and star floated thru the outside galaxy. The creator asked a question, he asked how would you feel if you had your own world inside of Lucy's room, they all got over excited, The creator explained to them what family was and the importance of the protection of family what we call unity and Loyalty here on Earth, he explained that aliens are not of him and that they are alienated away from him, because they chose to rebel, I do not give you a spirit of fear and I will not give you more than you can bear witness to, I am a zealous God, I am the morning sun, evening set, and the light of the night I am the word, and the word is me. The creator than turned to Lucy and said you are no longer the light bearer of the outside universe, I showed you genuine love nothing more nothing less, I love you so much Lucy that instead of punishing you I will reward you with your own world, where you are the prince of the air, take whoever you want with you, after manipulating a third of the outside universe, some stars actually were convinced that Lucy can do exactly what the creator can do and has done, so they followed her into her world where they were never allowed to come back from, Before Lucy left to go back to her room, her world where she was the prince of the air, Lucy felt beyond angry and over ruled by the creators decision, she balled up for 6 days to herself, 6 nights, in the last 6 hours, 6minutes, and 6 seconds…

Of the 6th day, Lucy was fully charged what we call rested. She was trying to become completely balanced, but instead Lucy became 3 protons 6 neutrons 6 electrons making Lucy a negative, Only the creator had authority to go into the energy chamber, Lucy came back to the outside galaxy for the very last time got one last look took her people and fled to never return in the beginning we were here…

ENERGY CHAMBER

Chapter 7

Now the only thing left in the outside universe was the creator and the called and chosen few, at this point the creator felt balance, not a piece of confusion in the air, the creator called forth his 12 engineers, they did not have free will. Nor did they have intention on wanting it... true dedicated soldiers, that would submit their entire soul to the will of the creator, of doing his good deeds, at this point the creator seen everything as Good, the entire outside universe was better than b4, the creator stood up and walked across the outside universe, it took the creator 12 steps to walk there and 12 steps to walk back, when the creator returned he took his 12 engineers into the energy chamber and taught them about Life and the importance of Life's journey, when they came out of the energy chamber, they had the strength of 24g, twenty-four little god's in one, the creator commanded that each engineer find one special starlet, and give him the teachings that he had blessed them with... once the teachings were completed with each starlet the creator lined them up 12 seats to his right, and 12 seats to his Left making a total of 24 engineers, the creator called them the 24 elders, the creator than began to explain to his 24 elders, I have given each of you a piece of me, I have given each of you and individual assignment, I have fulfilled your complete temple with a like mind of myself, a temple of genuine love, if one of my elders decide to break my command of no free will they shall be punished to never even know they had any existence, the 24 elders fully understood, at this point everything was seen as good in the creators eyes.

The creator called forth the attention of every star and starlet in the Universe, A Starlet is a smaller version of a star, used as a helper to a star in the outside universe, every starlet was assigned to a star. All stars, and starlet's were made in the image of the creator, compared to the creator, they were the size of an ant to a human, the 24 engineers were a lot stronger and taller than the other stars An starlet's and about a quarter of the Creator's body.

The creator than had the main 12 engineers line up across the entire outside universe, while he sat in the middle, he called forth His 2 brightest Stars Michael, and Gabrielle, and asked them to sing from the bottom of there hearts because a good thing had been done, The universe was at a standstill of amazement, the Creator began to explain the reason why he had to band little Lucy from the Outside Universe, what we would call heaven here on Earth. He opened His mouth and said I am nor masculine nor feminine, I am nor man, nor woman, I am The God over all creations, just because I created you does not make you one of mine, but the one's with a sound mind, of love and genuine happiness and obedience belongs to me. Any other thoughts are alienated away from me, I choose not to see disobedience, for I want to remember you as I created you of pure innocence and genuine love, why must you praise another god b4 me, for I am 10x's more powerful than the average Star And little g that I of the outside universe created. I am the Creator of the Father, The woman, and the wound she carries. The creator of the entire outside and inside universe, and the creator of the Eye of Life that see's, hears and knows everything, there's literally nothing you can get pass the universe.

The creator began to explain to the Stars there duty's while visiting Lucy's magnificent room, and explained to them the betrayal they just witnessed, and what they would have to go thru while visiting Lucy's room the creator told them the name of Lucy's room is called Earth, it was my own little farm, that means a lot to me and must be taken care of not destroyed, and our job was to go there and protect his farm from being destroyed, he promised us protection from the evil doings of Lucy and fallen stars what we call angels here on Earth, b4 the creator made another announcement about there duties on Earth, he allowed Michael and Gabrielle to take over the heavens as he went back into the energy chamber. when he came back the creator started to peep weird behavior coming from some of the starlets, the starlets were gaining knowledge and power, becoming a Lil more alert as the stars were, the creator turned his back to the outside universe, and just sat there in deep thought, Michael flow forth and said Father the Creator of all the heavens, stars, and starlets, why do you mourn, the creator replied after all of this, there are still 3 stars trying to find away to gain more knowledge than me that I created, and more strength that I created, after all of this they still try to betray me, the creator stayed with his back turned to the universe for 4 days, an 3 nights Earth time, during those 4 days of being absent the creator returned with a smile that lit up every star and starlet outside of the universe,

Chapter 8

Michael came to the creator and said do you see all of those starlets over there by that energy chamber? The creator responded and said yes why are they over there, Michael said 3 of the Stars led them to it, the stars told them that Lucy said the creator did not want them to gain a conscious and that all they had to do was disobey him and go see for yourself, so one starlet went and seen for itself, and came back and grabbed a few more, than they went back and got a few more, b4 you knew it once again 25% of the outside galaxy that was left circled around the energy chamber and tried to take it over as if it was there's. They said Lucy is smarter and more truthful than the creator because he didn't tell them that they would gain consciousness and left them to remain unconscious, but b4 the creator can get a chance to even explain anything to the Stars and starlets, they took it upon there self to betray An follow Lucy's orders.

Now at this point Lucy thought that by leaving behind a few tellers, what we would call spy's or snitches here on Earth, that her wicked manipulative plan would work and she would be allowed to take over the entire outside universe that the creator created. The creator and the 24 elders just stood there lined up across the universe in complete silence along with Michael and Gabrielle, as the 3 teller stars and the other 25% of the starlets started to sing and dance around the energy chamber with there gold chest plates stuck out as if they were ready for war, a full year had passed Earth years as the betrayed stars An starlets hovered around the energy ball, at this point the other starlets had became stars and were no longer starlets they were brighter and stronger, the creator noticed a movement from one of his elders, a movement of agitation, remember the elders don't have free will they can't act nor do without the command of the creator. The creator got ready to punish one of his elders but rite b4 he did that one of his bright stars, the brightest of them all Gabrielle started to drift towards the energy chamber, when Gabrielle got there, the other Stars were giggling, laughing, mocking, and taunting Gabrielle as he stood there with a firm look on his face, Gabrielle opened his mouth for the first time without singing and said why do you laugh and mock me and the creator, one of the 3 tellers stood up and said we laugh because your weak and the creator is not truthful, so Gabrielle smirked, the teller looked at Gabrielle and said why do you smile, Gabrielle opened his mouth and said I know a someone that can destroy this big ball of energy chamber you feel you have power over, the other Stars and tellers started to laugh At Gabrielle and said go get your creator and have him try, Lucy's our most high, Gabrielle smirked again, the other tellers and stars were starting to get agitated with Gabrielle, Gabrielle looked at the tellers and called one of them by there name he said Damon, do you not believe that this sword I possess in my hand can destroy this big ball of energy chamber? The teller Damon laughed and looked at Gabrielle with a serious sneaky look and said I would like for you to try, Gabrielle looked at Damon back with the same look and said you've never seen a storm before would you like to see one, Damon looked and said there's no way possible you or any other star outside of the universe can destroy this energy chamber, not even with the power of the creator.

Chapter 9

Gabrielle stood there firm, looked at Damon and said what's done outside of the universe does not have to be explained, Gabrielle flee'd away from Damon and the rest of the Stars an other 2 tellers, and grabbed a baby starlet, drifted back over to the energy chamber and handed the baby starlet the glowing shining stick that we would call a sword here on Earth, and looked at Damon and said to the lost, I will lift my voice and say this one time the creator loves you, and he's all about timing, I will give those a chance to be forgiven for the betrayal of the creator, only if you leave that ball now and come with Love, Gabrielle began to sing all of the stars were at amazement The 3 tellers stood up and laughed at the amazing gift that was given to Gabrielle, while they were laughing the baby starlet had snuck all the way up on the energy chamber, raised his stick as high as he can and went down hard stabbing the big ball of energy chamber, the starlet stood there with the sword inside of the energy chamber, but nothing seemed to happen the stars started to laugh even louder and taunt the starlet but the starlet never moved after about 5 hours Earth time of straight laughter and taunting, the energy chamber began to move a slight crack had began to form in the center of the ball that moved around the entire energy chamber, then all of a sudden the energy chamber split in half, and crumbed to pieces... large pieces of a metal formed rock made of Gold and silver, because of the

Faith that Damon, the stars and the other 2 tellers had in the big energy chamber ball that the creator had made, they began to disintegrate, all of them except the 3 tellers, Gabrielle then looked at Damon and said do you still feel that Lucy is brighter than your creator, Damon looked in amazement, then his amazement turned to fear, Gabrielle then looked at Damon and said fear is not allowed here, you shall join Lucy and the rest of her problems in her world, your name is no longer Damon, for the demon that possesses you has not been seen as good in my eyes, the 24 elder eyes, nor the creator's eyes... you 3 must flee and never return, for your Loyalty belongs to Lucy, when you return back to her, explain to her the power you witnessed of the creator outside of the universe, and explain that Lucy is no longer her name, her new name is NATAS, for she is looked at as Satan the fallen angel in the eyes of the creator, she is no longer Lucifer the light bearer for she has become dark, for he sees no good deeds, but a bad thing, and In the creator's eyes it's seen as no good. B4 Earth we were here.

DAMON THE DEMON

Chapter 10

At this point, the entire universe was in amazement for a good thing had been done, for the first time in a long while, the outside universe was at peace, all positive vibes celebrating, the baby starlet that stuck the shining stick into the energy chamber and destroyed it was rewarded a position, with a choice of free will, the creator seen a good thing had been done and named him Robert the Angel of death. Even the down spirited angel of death Robert better known as the reaper, soul snatcher, was celebrating. Robert didn't have free will as a starlet, he played a role as a servant to a star, he was created to be a downer spirit and to come drag the soul out of the lost, the creator created Robert, to gather the souls onto the space trip, to return them back to be present with him, rather its judgement or death, Robert was in control of gathering all of the lost souls after they left the physical body. Robert the reaper, the angel of death was created from darkness, he was giving free will to go wherever he wanted to across the inside universe what we call Earth, he was able to visit and check on anyone he wanted to, his only love was towards the creator, he had no respect a person, and had the power of 12 stars in one, he was much powerful, but only did the will of the creator, the creator sent Robert the death angel down to NATAS beautiful world, the creator's farm, his special place, Robert's assignment was to find the 3 teller's, and make them work for him as spy's.

Meanwhile, The Creator that we know as Father, quickly quieted down the outside universe, the Creator stood up tall, and started to reintroduce himself, he referred to himself as (I AM) The creator looked at every star and starlet outside of the universe, and said I AM the Alpha and Omega, The beginning and the end, I AM the creator of existence, and the creator of Death, the creator of life, and the creator of the afterlife, I AM, that I AM, that I AM.

Every Star looking in amazement over excited about the victory, every star but one, the creator peeped the confused look on one of the stars face, he asked, why must you look so confused shouldn't you be proud, and filled with joy, and celebrating with the rest of the outside universe? The star replied I'm going to miss Lucy's voice, but I won't miss her down spirit, I always wanted to sing like Lucy, and shine as bright as Lucy, that's why I followed her to her world but when she told us to come with her forever Lucy told me I would never be accepted into her world my soul is just as weak as the creator, when Lucy told me that I was spirit broken, I felt down for the first time, and felt a condemned feeling, a feeling of something I shouldn't have done, I don't wanna feel lost anymore, every stars happy but me, and I don't know why said the star. The creator than asked Gabrielle to bring that star to the front, Gabrielle put the star in front of the entire outside galaxy which would be a number bigger than a trillion. The creator looked at the star and said everyday a star is being born, everyday a star is being created, everyday a star is being held and covered by me, the new stars in the North are my chosen stars, the new stars in the east are my intelligent Stars, the stars to the west are my warrior stars, and the stars to the south point are my called stars, the stars that will help enlighten the non-enlightened, easily persuaded stars. B4 Earth we were here...

Chapter 11

The creator began to break the outside galaxy down into what he would call star gates, the star gates were broken down into century's, and generations, based on the order each star was made in, he then sat every star in the outside galaxy down, and said who would like to play a game in Lucy's world, every star agreed to play the game, everyone was excited, and not a piece of fear were in them. The Creator assigned each generation to one of the 24 elders, each engineer was assigned their own energy chamber, every star got a chance to take the test with the engineers, the test broke the stars down into zodiac signs, and assigned each star a number, the test the stars took showed how smart they were, how strong they were, and how different they were, the test also proved if you were masculine or feminine, man or woman, the first 24 stars that entered into the energy chamber came out with sense of humors, all of them excited, they were stationed to a waiting area outside the universe until the other stars were completed with their first test with the elders, the test allowed you to taste, feel, hear, and see, the test even allows you to experience the sensational feeling of mating, how it feels to procreate.

After every entire star in the outside universe was tested, they were then assigned away from the waiting area to their star gate, once the Stars got situated into their star gate, the creator stood up and assigned arch angels, the arch angels test were way above the average score of the rest of these stars, these stars were considered not just Angels but arch Angels, that was rewarded with bright halo's. He assigned each arch angel to a star gate. They were the leaders of each star gate, the arch Angels were told to choose a captain of each team once that was done they reported back to the creator, the creator than stood again and opened up his voice and said Let the games began.

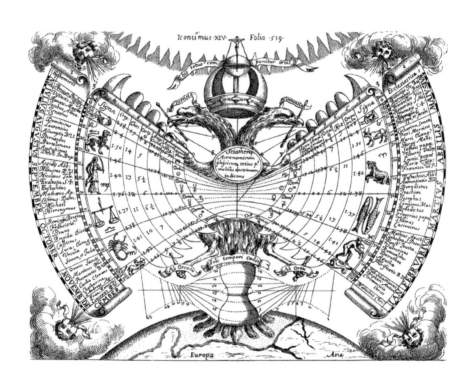

Chapter 12

The games broke down each star gates team skills, teaching them unity and loyalty, and teaching them to work with their brother and sister, the games were coming to an end, it came down to the last two star gates, the creator came up with his decision of the winner of the games, the star-gates the creator picked first he placed them last, the star-gates that were fighting there hardest for first place but got last he placed them first, the star-gates that finished first and were placed last were again confused at the creator's decision, one of the stars asked the creator why must you place us last, did we not do a good thing? Were you not pleased? The creator laughed showing his sense of humor, he then said what's done does not need to be explained, but I'd rather show you the outcome results, trust me and know I will always be there even if you can't see me, every star smiled and felt the feeling of being covered as if someone threw a warm blanket on you. A feeling of knowing that they were secure,

The creator opened his voice and said absent with the body is present with the creator, he then began to say the first shall be last, and the last shall be first. For I am the word and the word is good. Each star gate had 1 trillion stars in it, there were 24 star gates, 24 elders assigned to each one that would be an estimate of about 24 trillion stars, remember everyday a generation of called stars was born, every month a generation of chosen few stars were born, Earth time and the creator's time are not on the same time, even me the author can only guess his times, even after being there spiritually with the creator seeing this vision Clear as day, I remember waking up looking at myself in amazement, knowing I was somewhere else, somewhere spiritual, I even had a good feeling when I woke up, in shock of how real and beautiful that place was. I still never seen how much time it actually took for the creator to get to this point, he only showed me flashes of the events, he didn't show me what happened or occurred in between the events. He allowed me to see this just as clear as you can see a picture on the TV screen in 3D.

When I was younger my father's mother which is my grandmother used to read the Bible to me as a child, and would explain each story to me, along with each character and their position, she was a Baptist, my mother's father which is my grandfather, used to read the Quran to me and explain the interesting stories to me and each characters purpose, my aunt and uncle were Buddhist, they taught me about meditation, I took all the good out of each religion and brought it together and found that there were truths in all religions, the creator gave me a gift of discernment to see through the negativity and false arguments.

I remember standing next to the creator as he took me as I fell back sound asleep, I woke up in the spiritual world again, the creator had left off, The creator quieted down the outside universe, and said I love each and every last one of you with every piece of me that I used to make me, I know each and every one of you personally for I the father created you, and gave you a piece of my sense of humor. The creator the grand architect pulled up an image of a human being male and female, and broke the human body down in front of us, as clear as if you were staring at yourself in the mirror, the creator showed us Earth, showed us animals, food, water, land, wind, cars, houses, jets, planes, even UFO's, all of the stars were over excited. The creator then took me to the North wing, where all of the chosen stars were, over to the right standing there was me, before I even knew that I would become who I am, next to me in my star-gate were people I know, people I see every day, from coworkers to family to friends, to associates and familiar faces that I've passed before here on Earth, I was amazed I looked at the creator and smiled and said we were always with each other, we already knew each other b4 we came here, wow, I was over excited to see my family members and friends right there next to me in my star-gate, the creator looked at me and smiled, I asked the creator why do you choose to show me this, he responded and said Gregory I find you very bright for I see a good thing, I smiled even bigger than I did before, he said come take a walk with me, he took me to Earth and alone the sand and water he walked with me, he asked me to look deep into the sea and tell him what do I see, I replied life, and he answered correct, by staring at the sea the sky and what you call life, you're looking at me, and the wind is my presence. He then asked me to open my voice and sing, I did as he pleased, I tried to stop singing and he looked at me and smiled and said, let me take u somewhere else, he then took me in front of the universe I saw myself as a star, leading a choir I had the voice of a child, that shined just as bright as Lucy.

Chapter 13

the creator looked at me and said you are the new light bearer, and Lucy knows who you are, she's very envious of you because I see a good thing in you, but know need to have fear, I don't give you that feeling but the feeling of power and anointance, for every demon and negative spirit will fear your anointance.

I remember back when I was a child, I was around 9 or 10 years old, my grandfather called me to visit him in prison at the Pontiac correctional center where he was in-prisoned and stripped of his rights, he explained to me that this is no place for no man, and the only way he's making it thru, is because of the power of Allah, my grandfather was a Muslim, his name was William Hassan Abdul Abree, my grandfather and his close Muslim friend which was also an inmate on death row along with my grandfather, his name was Mario Flores. They gave me a Muslim name, they named me Lil Ali, Abdul Abree... they told me I was a warrior, a called messenger from God, and that a true Muslim was a true Christian, they den proceeded to tell me about religion and the separation it causes, and that Allah is not the author of confusion, although many Muslims believe Muhammad was the last great prophet to walk the Earth, in reality there's many Muhammad's and many Jesus's, still living to this day, my grandfather and his friend began to explain to me, that I was one of them, and that I am a modern day Muhammad and a modern day Jesus/ Yashua. They began to read to me other stories from Greek mythology, to the sun God, to Buddha, to monks, they even broke down to me the meaning of astrology and numerology, I remember being very excited and eager to hear and learn more, it was time to go, my grandfather kissed the top of my head and giggled, looked me in my eyes and said the creator has chosen me, and that I must go thru with the oath, he looked at me with a deep firm look in my eyes and told me, never fear anything for the creator does not give you that spirit of fear, and to live my life accordingly to the good deeds of the creator. This was a direct confirmation from the creator himself, I soaked it all up and took it all in. B4 Earth we were here...

Chapter 14

I remember the day it started, the day I was born again, the day I woke up in heaven. I used to always hear rumors that when a person dies that they always see a bright white light, that's what I was looking for, but instead I seen different, b4 I even got a chance to find the light, it was complete darkness, with the worst smell you can ever smell in your life, more worse than the smell of a rotten egg, underneath a sewer, it was the worst smell I have ever encountered in my life. It was better to hold your breath and not breathe than to breathe at all... I remember being surrounded in pitch darkness, waiting for my night vision to kick in, but it never did, at this point a feeling of fear had come over me, a feeling of being lost and knowing I would never see any one of my loved ones ever again, I remember trying to walk thru the darkness but every-time I tried to move I felt a pinch all over my body, every step I took the pinches got even harder than b4, the pain was so terrible I just stood there, waiting for a tear to fall but it never did, at this point I knew I was dead, and that I was a lost soul in hell, I began to pray calling on the creator, asking him to please take me away from this evil place, my soul can't take this pain, as I began to pray and call on the help of the creator, he sent an angel to me, the angel looked at me in disgust and told me this is not to punish you but to show you the values of life. I asked the angel can he take me away from this evil place I don't wanna be here anymore, I can't stand another second breathing down here. The angel looked at me and said no but I know someone who can, why do you have so much faith in me, when I'm only an angel, I looked at the angel and said because I know your close to my father, for I've been down here and seen nothing but darkness, and the voice of millions of lost souls crying out, there sins, saying they'll never do it again. For this type of darkness that I witness is evil, and not seen as good in my eyes, for the light that I saw from you gave me hope, that I can be saved from this place, the angel then looked at me and smirked, he waved his hand across my vision and I woke up coming into a light, as if I was coming thru a triangular wound being born again, as if a mother was having a new born baby.

Before I came out of that triangular wound, the triangle opened up into a Square, I entered into the light of the square, and b4 I can see anything I heard a strong voice say come to me, for I see balance in you, when you were in the wound you were safe but confused as you were entering into a triangular wound of light… But the confusion did not make you scared nor have fear, that's what made you balanced in my eyes for your fourth eye is now open. You must not add to nor take away from my word, for you are chosen and I have called you, to not only be a great leader, but to show the world how to turn away from there evil and no good ways, thru the great teachings of your creator, for I have put you thru the hardest struggles, tested your faith, and allowed your path to be crooked, b4 I allowed you to get back on track, and make your path straight again.

I have seen a good thing in you, I have chosen you to carry on this oath, for I know you can change the minds of the lost. A wise man knows a man that think he knows everything, knows nothing, and a man that admits he knows nothing is a man that's willing to learn. For I am the creator of all creations, and the author of truth, for your ways are not my ways, and your evil wondering thoughts are not my thoughts, for the flesh is weak, and I look for the strong that can control the weak. I am no punk says the creator, neither do I expect my people to be, the position that I give to you is for you, I do not expect for other people to act out as you, but to walk like you, in the righteous heart of the creator, for your heart is seen as good, for your good outweigh the bad, that's why I see the best in you, son. By having your good deeds outweigh your bad deeds it allows your spirit to light up a room, and allows me to see the light still shinning bright in you, the light that shines in you is known as the Holy Spirit, and the Holy Spirit allows me to know everything is seen as good.

B4 Earth we were here...

Chapter 15

I than remember a spirit floating up to me, his image was transparent, but his facial features were seeable, with the prettiest bluish gold glow coming from its features. The spirit approached me and said come to me, this spirit had the features of my grandfather who had passed away, my spiritual teacher that had opened me up to life, and was given life in prison, behind the spirit was a long line of other spirits with features that looked like mine, all ages, I asked the spirit who are those spirits, and why are they looking at me confused, the spirit replied and said those are your ancestors, and you're not supposed to be here yet, this is in between it's called purgatory. After the spirit told me that, a feeling of excitement came over my body, I then looked to the left and it was a line full of young spirits, with the image of children in a transparent body, they were all excited to get on this machine that looked like a roller coaster, the children were entering into it and I was curious and over excited about seeing what the machine did and why the other spirits were so overly excited. I then heard the spirit call me again and told me to come to him, but instead I went to the left where the other excited spirits were, when I got there these spirits were people I knew, people that I haven't met on Earth but spirits I was around b4 I came to Earth, I knew these spirits by names, better than I know my family, I was excited to see them and they were excited to see me as if I had gone out of town somewhere and

I was just coming back, the spirits boosted me to the front of the line and allowed me to go next, I entered into the machine and two spirits strapped me in, they closed the machine and I started to fly as fast and as high as I wanted to, in this machine were other spirits excited like me, in between not having no worries we were all flying, inside of the machine was another long line, this line had spirits lined up to go to war, this station was called the rapture war games, with a huge sign with the picture of Gabrielle the arch angel on it, these spirits new who I were too and I knew them by names, they flew me to the front of the line, I entered into the machine inside of the machine, and in this machine was a look of the last days, you had a choice to choose the gold team or the blue team, I chose the gold team, the object of the game was to drag as many Demons as we can to the dungeon, we had long glow in the dark Star Wars looking sticks along with transparent laser guns as if we were playing laser tag, but this world aloud you to feel pain if you got shot or stabbed, a real experience of how it feels to go to war, after we picked our weapons we entered into a huge dome with horses and chariots we were allowed to pick our horses all the male horses were black with wings, all the female horses were white with black wings and a gold unicorn the prettiest creature you can ever imagine, these horses had a soul, and were built for war, 10x's the size of a regular horse, imagine horses the size of 3 giraffes in one. The horses did not have free will in the games, but had to submit to the spirit that chose to ride it. The spirits on my team all flew together, we flew from the heavens next to the horse that was assigned to us, down to the destroyed cruel world of Natas. The game was to destroy everything moving, for everything left on Earth was seen as no good in the creator's eyes, we had the key to destroy, the games was coming to an end and my team was losing, I remember hopping on my black horse, looking for more spirits, but instead came across This little girl hiding behind a mountain, I flew to her, she was balled up as if she knew I was going to destroy her, I smelled and felt fear all over her, but I couldn't detect a soul, at this point I became confused as I walked up to the little girl she wept, and begged for me not to destroy her or take her back to the dungeon, she told me she has the key to give me everlasting life on Earth only if I didn't turn her in or destroy her, the little girl stood up with a very sad look on her face, and waved her hand across my vision, when she did that it took me away from the games it took me to an empty room with nothing but a table and a bright light as if I was at a hospital, I remember seeing glass see through walls and glass see through floors and ceilings, I was laying on a table with 3 people standing over me shining a bright light in my face to the point where I couldn't see their face, I tried to ask where I was, but they ignored me as if I wasn't even there, I felt a hand push my head back and then waved their hand across my vision, I then woke up in a room with a girl sitting across from me, she looked confused I asked her if she knew where we were, she calmly said no, then came and sat next to me and laid on me, man, that was the most comfortable feeling ever, this girl was beyond beautiful, before Earth we were here…

Chapter 16

This girl was so beautiful and sweet that I would've given up everything to spend the rest of my life with her. She seemed to know me as if she knew exactly who I was, at this point I was trying to remember where I knew her from as if my memory had gotten erased, she began to laugh and joke with me, telling me stories that I did before that I remembered but didn't remember living those moments on Earth.

She laid under me and told me her deepest secrets, she told me she was born with no vision, and that I was the first person she saw when she opened her eyes, she said the first thing she had seen was a bright triangular light, once she chose to go thru the light she tried to open her eyes and seen nothing, she said she was just there, feeling lost and empty for a very long time, with no hope of ever being saved, she looked up at me and called me her savior, she told me I was her god, and that she was my goddess, I became confused, I looked at her and before I can ask her what she mean by that, she waved her hand across my vision, I woke back up on a table with the bright light back in my face, I got tired of that light shining in my face and getting ignored, I turned my head to the right and thru the clear glass walls I seen spirits lined up excited as if they were about to go on vacation, these spirits were feminine, allowing me to know that they were women. Getting ready to get stationed into their star-gate before entering Earth. Some of the spirits in line were pointing at me, as if where I was laying on the table was a good thing, I then remember hearing a loud beep from the machine as if they were about to shock my heart to revive me. I then looked and walking down the hall was that same spirit I was in the room with, it seemed as if I had a crush all over again, but I couldn't speak nor move, she was walking with another spirit with a clip board in her hand floating pass the clear glass hallways, she looked back but didn't wave, I seen a hand wave across my vision again, I woke back up in that room again, I looked at the spirit that was there with me, and asked her where was she going and why didn't she try to speak to me, she put her head down and said I love you with every piece of me that the creator used to make me, and I don't want you to leave my world, I than put my head down, she walked up to me and said we will never be what you want us to be for you are no longer my god and I am no longer your goddess. Your intentions is only after lusting for me. She than waved her hand across my vision I woke back up in the room with the light in my face, the light was slightly removed from in front of my face, and the three people standing over me faces were blurry I couldn't tell nor see who they were, I than turned my head to the right and seen the girl from my dream world floating pass again, this time she looked at me as she was floating by, she was holding hands with another male spirit, he looked identical to my earthly features, I imagined it was me in another dimension, I was heartbroken, as if I got cheated on with a clone of myself. At this point I felt jealous, hurt, and betrayed, she told me all of her deepest secrets, she trusted me, and comforted me, just to walk away as if she never knew me, at this point I didn't trust a soul. As She floated by holding hands with the spirit that looked like me, I smiled as she waved at me, I seen a hand go across my vision again, I woke back up in the room, she was there, this time she was happy, she confessed that the creator had not only given her sight but he had given her a vagina and turned her spirit into a woman. At this point I didn't know what to believe, she told me I had helped her past her test, and the creator seen the best in her, and that her heart was seen as good, but then she put her head down and said but a woman is not what I wanted to be, but because I found the first thing I seen attractive which was a male spirit, and submitted my heart to you, made us soul mates, you helped me find myself, she kissed my forehead and before I can look up and try to hug her back, she attempted to wave her hand across my vision, I stopped her from doing it, I than looked at her, and said is the love real, I'm not leaving again until I know it's real…. but she couldn't answer, and started to act weird as if she had somewhere to go as if she was trying to flee from me, my spirit sensed something wasn't right so I looked at her and grabbed her, and said this is what real love feels like, I instantly woke up, back on the table with the light in my face I turned my head and waited for her to walk back down that hallway with the guy that looked like me… trying to prepare myself to accept the fact that she didn't belong to me, as I laid there looking I seen them come floating down the clear glass hallways, with a piece of paper in her hand this time the male spirit didn't have the clip board.

Chapter 17

The male spirit handed her another piece of paper that said game over, she looked at me and a tear dropped as she smiled, and whispered I'm free. Thank you, at this point I was happy but still confused of where I was, I was just happy that I helped better someone, than I started to think as I laid there why would she tell me I'm no longer her god and she's no longer my goddess, and why would she refer to me as her savior, than as I was thinking that, the light removed completely from in front of me, I seen a face, the face of an angel, staring at me with the same features as the girl from that room that I had fell in love with, she opened her mouth and answered the question that I was thinking, she said because you helped Natas find a piece of love, you've made her weaker, and every time a spirit defeats her manipulation game, she gets even weaker, the next manipulation game Natas starts to play with another spirit she won't be as wise as she was before. By showing love you allowed Natas to become weaker, and because you stopped her from being less heartless, when she was stopping you from waking back up in that room, you allowed her to expose herself to you, you broke Natas down, love is what defeats her, because of this good doing, you just put the gold team in first place, you didn't know it, but all the people who pushed you to the front of the line where all people who once doubted you, but once it was exposed to them that you were chosen, the simple minded spirits looked at you different in amazement, and depended on you, and in the games each team picks a chosen god and a chosen goddess to defeat Natas, in her own world, congratulations your team has won, she than waved her hand across my face, and I was standing there with every spirit in purgatory celebrating congratulating me for doing a good deed. An angel flew up to me and through his wing over my head and waved his feathers across my vision, my eyes were all the way open walking out of the rapture games. I remember floating back up to that spirit that looked like my grandfather, I finally decided to go over there to him, but I couldn't get close to him, every time I tried to go to him the further away from me he got, he looked at me and smirked and said nothing, I got to a point where I felt real stiff and couldn't move as if something was holding me down in my sleep and I couldn't awake, everything got real dark, and that feeling of fear started to come back towards me, at this point I was afraid to move, expecting to feel those horrible deep pinches again all over my body, hoping I don't smell that horrible disgusting smell again. But this time I wasn't by myself it was 6 others there with me, with just enough night vision to see something moving, they were all looking confused as I was, than I heard a male voice say did anyone else die in their sleep besides me, because this has to be death what else can this place be that we woke up in, than I heard a female say I was driving, I don't remember hitting anything, I just remember waking up here, I must've gotten in a car accident, than I heard another voice say, I was drinking than I remember feeling real weak almost as if I was too sick to move, I just remember laying by a big garbage can balled up, and waking up here, oh man, this must be hell, something told me to get my life right and I didn't listen, than I said my name is Greg last thing I remember before I woke up in all kind of different places is I was at my apartment complex and 6 people came to my crib to do a home invasion, I remember 6 people with shirts over there face trying there hardest to kill me, I remember fighting back calling on the lord as they stabbed me multiple times to the body hitting me in my head with hammers and guns, stabbing me in my neck, and the back of my head, I remember feeling no pain as if someone laid on my back and took the pain from me as I called on Jesus, I fought them off and the door popped open and pushed all 6 of them to my back wall, as they were trying to kill me they were chanting Cha, cha, cha, kill him, cha, cha, cha, kill him, I thought that was beyond weird, and I saw this tall bald guy magically appear in my house as if he was the devil himself there watching them do it, as I was fighting for my life calling on the lord, the door popped open I remember thinking this the last thing I'm finna see before I die a door and a wall, I got up and ran down the hallway, and I heard a gun go off and a force pushed me to the ground, I looked back and seen a broken hammer, in my head oh they just threw a hammer at my back it didn't register that I had got shot in the back, I just thought it was a hard blow from the hammer getting thrown at me, I looked back and seen a hammer on the ground and it was broken, in my head they threw a hammer at my back so I stood up and turned and faced all 6 of them and just looked as blood rushed from the top of my head to the soul of my feet.

Chapter 18

They looked at me confused and ran out the emergency exit door, across from my apartment, I ran to the laundry room there was a girl in there washing clothes she looked at me and passed out, I instantly hit the stairway and was trying to breathe both of my lungs were busted at this point, I hit the stairway and got ready to run up the stairs, but it felt like something lifted me and glided me up the stairs from the 1st floor to the 6th floor something knocked on my guy d mac's door he's 6'5 I'm 6'2 when d mac opened the door he said I was taller than him I fell on his shoulder with blood everywhere I remember being on the elevator and d mac screaming at me saying you bet not die on me. I remember gasping for air as if you hit a cigarette to hard and trying not to cough. The first time I coughed my body had gave up, and the first time I woke up I was here, the second place they took me was purgatory, and now I'm back here again, and this is no place for no spirit.

B4 Earth we were here.

A angel appeared and said fear not, for the creator does not give you a spirit of fear, a voice said loudly, why are we here than, cause I'm beyond scared in this place, than another voice said the creator isn't real, when you die everybody comes to this place, welcome to hell... when I heard that voice say that, I looked at the shinning angel and knew it was hope, that was the same angel I encountered before, so I felt warm and safe when he appeared. The angel only grabbed 3 out of the 7 people that came and said follow me, the angel was the only light in that horrible dark place, we followed him for about 10 minutes through a dark smelly tunnel there was another door leading to another tunnel this tunnel was full of cages and jail cells with people in them, with transparent flesh hanging off of their bodies, they were mocking the angel as he guides us through the tunnel, A woman opened her voice and said why do these people taunt you? Why do they taunt the creator calling him a false God why? With an angry look on her face, the angel turned and said why do you rise your eyebrows with anger? The woman replied because I don't like what they're doing, the angel than replied and said what is your name, the woman replied Mary, the angel said marry hold your question for these people have rebelled and are not of the creator, they belong to Natas, even after knowing she's a master manipulator, some of the people here still feels there's hope with their savior Natas whom they call Satan.

As the angel guided us down the two dark tunnels we were approaching another tunnel ahead, the angel stopped at the end of the second tunnel and said fear not for the next tunnel is dark and full of fire, I can't enter pass this tunnel or I would be punished, I don't know what's ahead the creator won't allow me to know neither do I have any concerns on what's down there. You may enter at will if you choose not to go your mission will be aborted, one stayed now it was just me and the woman floating to the next tunnel, at this point as we were floating not a piece of fear came over my body, as I was floating I started to see a light in the middle of the tunnel I got excited again, as we approached the light a voice said fear not, for I am a messenger, known to you as Jesus Christ, or Yashua. I am close to the creator just as close as you are, you've observed my ways, and kept a strong firm love for our father, for I am yah your brother, for I came to Earth first and witnessed the wicked ways of the world, even myself admits the flesh is weak, but still possible to be self-controlled, you have free will, make your free will the right choices, and you will forever be blessed, and our father the creator will never take his hand off of you. I was 33 when I ascended into the outside universe, what you know as heaven, you Gregory are 33 years old, for me it was the ending of a new beginning, for you this is the beginning, when I was killed, murdered by the lost, I planted seeds as I ascended and planted them all over the world, right now, your seed has been watered, and your glass is full of knowledge and wisdom, this is a gift for the lost to see that you can't be stopped because of the anointance that has been placed upon you, I will use you to put every demonic wicked wise man who think he knows, who knows nothing to shame. For the creator is a perfect timing God, and is always on time, for the first shall be last, and the last shall be first, he began to explain to me that Lucy has always been this way, every since she was created, the creator new that if he gave Lucy enough power to feel she was as strong as him, that she would eventually try to overrule him, what Lucy doesn't know is that a smart mind can play dumb, but a dumb mind can't play smart, Lucy has thrown temper tantrums since the beginning, before the creator had created the entire outside universe, what we call aliens here on Earth where all once spirits created by the creator living outside the universe what we call Heaven.

Chapter 19

B4 the beginning was the beginning, b4 the creator made the 10 engineers elders, there were already 2 loyal soldiers of the creator, Gabrielle and Michael, what we call aliens today on Earth where once angels, they were beyond intelligent, a magic trick would be a bad joke compared to the type of intelligence they had… they had the I-Q of ten Albert Einstein's in one, they were created to build and procreate, one day a crowd of aliens got together and decided that they wanted to build their own galaxy inside of the outside universe, the creator granted them there wishes, they told the creator that they didn't want him to see it b4 it was done, but once again a smart mind can play dumb but a dumb mind can't play smart, no matter how intelligent you think you are. You can never outsmart the creator, he doesn't use pieces he plays chess with spirits, hoping he can find someone that can one day give him a real match, without abusing their power he gave them, all of the aliens had free will at once upon a time, the creator allowed them to build another galaxy but no matter how hard they tried or how intelligent they were they could never build it nor design it how the creator structured the outside universe. The aliens started to get frustrated and very envious of the creator, because they couldn't get there world to form in the shape of the top of the creator's world, for century's the alienated angels were building trying to get it right, but never could, one day the head alien whose name was Damon handed down his rank as a high ranked star, and submitted to do the will of The creator, for he seen it was impossible to form his world how the creator did, Damon handed it over to a feminine spirit named Lilith, Lilith was strong and intelligent, Lilith shined brighter than any star outside the galaxy, the creator asked Lilith if she thought it was possible to form her galaxy how the creator did his, Lilith replied no it is not possible without the ways of you, Lilith was very beautiful, Lilith had formed her world almost like the creator did, Lilith world shined brighter than any star outside the galaxy but every star outside of the galaxy couldn't see it, it was the size of an ant to a human, the creator giggled and seen a good thing that Lilith had done, he rewarded her to bring anyone she'd like to her world, because her world shined so bright he named her the moon goddess, for he seen she was warm and at peace, as time and years outside the universe went by certain stars started to outgrow Lilith's world, so billions of stars left and went back to the outside universe, Lilith was becoming dark, and her light was starting to dim, she was becoming what you would call jealous here on Earth, she wanted to be the creator so bad, she had the aliens that where there start to build meteor weapons, these alienated stars, had enough technology to build a nuke meteor launcher to send shooting across ten galaxy's. The nuke meteor launcher also was used to make portals, that send you through different dimensions created by the creator, these dimensions where created for lucid dreaming, to give the conscious mind a place to learn and experience more of what he wanted them to know without speaking, it was hard to understand the creator when he spoke, his voice shook the whole outside universe, it sounded like the loudest thundering and lightning sound you can ever here, very frightening to someone in the flesh, getting orders from him, I guess that's why every time he began to speak he would send an high ranked star to deliver the message, and to tell every starlet in the outside galaxy to fear not. For his words bring peace, justice and satisfaction to the soul.

Lilith had all of the alienated stars line all of the meteor launcher's up and point directly at the top of the creator's outside universe, one of the teller starlets came to the most high ranked star Lilith and asked If he can be her main servant, As she was to the creator, Lilith looked at the starlet and said your heart is made like the creator's, Lilith picked the teller up and smiled at the teller starlet and broke his little wings, the starlet looked up to Lilith and loved her ways, and asked why do you break my wings are they not strong enough to fly with your high ranked stars, am I not beautiful enough, is my soul not pure enough, why must you punish me? At this point Lilith had became cruel, her light had officially died, because Lilith broke the wings of an innocent servant who was seen as pure in heart in the creator's eye's, Lilith did not get a chance to attempt to fire her meteor launcher at the top of the creator's outside universe.

Chapter 20

The creator new that Lilith was not capable of being a righteous leader, reason why he gave the position as the most high ranked star to Damon, he was strong and only wanted to know truths, But even Damon new to submit to the creator, and not to try to overrule him for he will be destroyed or punished, Lilith didn't care especially after her light burned out, it shut down every piece of light inside of her world, it became so dark only 25% of stars stayed the other 75% left to be back present in the creator's world, and they were easily accepted back into the outside universe.

The creator banned Lilith and the other 25% of the stars, and took his starlet's back to be re assigned to a star, he then sent Lilith and the other fallen angels wondering in the dark lost sunken galaxy to never return to the outside universe and named them aliens, for they were seen as rebellious, and very envious and jealous he loved Lilith so much that he didn't destroy her, but gave her, her own piece of darkness to travel through along with all of their creative intelligence that he blessed Lilith and the other fallen stars, and to never return back to the heavens, the outside universe. He placed Lilith and the other 25% inside of the galaxy to wonder in a sunken place they've never seen and know nothing about, on Earth we call that place outer space,

Meanwhile while Lilith and the other fallen stars were lost for millions of years wondering, trying to find a way back into the outside universe, even after all she did the Creator allowed Lilith to still be illuminated, enlightened by truth, since Lilith wanted to be the creator, he allowed her to wonder and build as they were created to do, but Lilith was restricted from going certain places, the creator told Lilith she can't come close to this special place of life we call Earth, and encounter with any living spirit he created, unless it's with the permission of me, that I will never give you, Lilith became even more disgusted with the creator, As time went by and century's passed by, Lilith and her other fallen stars found a way to discover technology, at this point they found a way to create light without the help of the creator, Lilith was really testing the creators patience, but once again a smart mind can play dumb but a dumb mind can't play smart, Lilith thought she had out smarted the creator, and decided to rebel and over rule his word, and attack his farm, meanwhile the creator sent the teller star down as a spy to bring back information and what was going on, and what Lilith plan was, one of Lilith's fallen stars spotted the teller star spying behind a huge rock, the fallen star immediately captured the teller starlet and took it Lilith the teller star told Lilith I'm loyal to you and the creator sent me as a spy, but I didn't have plans on going back, Lilith had her stars torture the starlet and do all kind of evil things to the starlet, the teller starlet returned with a down look on its face and said I told Lilith everything, how I was a spy, and how you sent me to spy on her and the other fallen stars, the creator rewarded the teller starlet, he made the teller a high ranked star, and removed the downer spirit that was living inside of it, he named this high ranked star Lucifer, for he seen something strong, and powerful in this high ranked star, for he seen a good thing and the creator had felt, this starlet had been through enough pain, and have had enough. This high ranked star was the light bearer of the outside universe, with a feminine spirit he nick named her Lucy. The creator than said, there was never nothing for you to tell on about Lilith, for there's nowhere for her to go in the inside universe, but down, the creator than said, I wanted her to torture you, I wanted her to see you in pain, for because she thought by hurting you, that it would hurt me, but instead I reward you with the same position I was going to give to her, now I want Lilith to see how strong you've became and how bright you are, lift your voice and sing Lucy for a good thing has been done, Lucy opened her voice and sang, she brought warmth to every star outside of the universe, b4 Earth we were here...

Chapter 21

Yah began to explain to me and the other spirit, that life is not exactly what it seems to be, but a grand stimulation for enlightenment, a grand stimulation that separates the good, and the bad, the light and the dark, a grand stimulation made out of love, and unity, any spirit with wrong doings is punished, no sin is bigger than the other, you get back what you give out.

Yah, began to explain that, because the law of the land is officially corrupt, you are now governed by the creator, the father of all creations himself, the creator knows you personally and pays very close attention to you to, he finds you interesting, in his eyes you 2 are seen as good, for that you shall remain rich in spirit. Yah looked at Mary and said there's something on your mind may I ask what it is? Mary replied why do you allow them to talk to you that way, why do you just allow them to taunt you? For you have the key to shut down the entire hell, Yah replied, these people would rather not exist than to be in this place of torment, these people know it's too late for them, Yah's wounds began to bleed, from his head, to his hands, to his rib, to the soul of his feet, one tear dropped down, she asked the creator why do he weep? He replied and said after all the wrong doings they've done, I still have a love for them like no other, just as the creator seen the best in you, he seen the best in me, the happier your soul, the higher ranked you would be. For the Creator sees through the soul, and judges the heart, it's either cold, or warm, for our heart matches the same, me and you are one, and so is every other warm hearted spirit allowing you to be one of his chosen one's. Mary are you not the same person who turned the homeless away from the church? Are you not the same woman that locked the doors during hurricane Katrina? Are you not the same one who judge every one you come across? Mary put her head down with a condemned sad look and said please forgive me, he then looked at Mary and said are you not the same person who judged every color including your own? Mary didn't reply, she stood there with a cold heart.

Yah then proceeded to take us to another part of hell, he explained to us there are many different levels of hell, just as there are many different levels of heaven, we walked to this tall dark door with a light coming from the cracks, we approached the door and opened it, inside were lost souls hanging from hooks with transparent flesh hanging off their bodies, almost as if they were zombies off of a movie, one of them spoke and said my savior save me, for my spirit can't handle this place, Yah wounds began to bleed again, and a tear dropped, Yah didn't reply. As the hooks spun around, Yah closed the door and proceeded going to the right of the dark door where there was another door with light coming from it, Yah wounds began to bleed even harder Yah asked us to take his hand, as we touched his hand the blood that was running down his hand cooled us down, for the heat down there was unbearable, he then took us to a lake, this lake looked as if we were on Earth, staring at Lake Michigan, but this lake didn't have water, this lake was full of fire with billions of lost souls in it all trying to get to shore, but every time they made it, these troll looking demons stabbed them with pitch forks allowing them to move away from shore, there were also human bat looking people with tore up wings with holes in them as if they were ripped, Mary looked at Yah and said I wanna go back, there's some people I have to ask for

63

forgiveness, there are some people that I've done wrong, that I've judged that I know I shouldn't have, there are people who I looked at that were family that I treated so badly, so wrong, whom I could've helped out but instead I watched them suffer, thinking I was making myself feel good, but instead I was dying in the inside, abusing my power working as a minister in the church, can you please forgive me and take me out of this place, the creator wounds began to bleed a nonstop flow as if his wounds was a river of blood.

Yah, looked at Mary and said, you've been forgiven ever since the first time your heart felt condemned. For in the spirit world what's done does not have to be explained for the creator knows your heart, just as well as I do, for the creator doesn't see color, but see's love in the pure in heart. For the creator is the creator of the word genuine, the creator of feeling the feeling of being genuine, the creator of love. For he doesn't see evil but see's the best in you. The lost souls in the lake of fire began to scream save us. Calling him every name they knew him of, in every different language, but Yah, closed the door to that level.

As we proceeded through another dark path way, there was a bright light illuminating the dark with its bright bluish gold light shining from it, standing there was the angel Michael.

DIFFERENT LEVELS OF HELL

Chapter 22

Michael grabbed Mary by the hand and took her away faster than the speed of lightning. Yah proceeded to take me to the master level of Hell, sitting on a thrown was Natas, sitting there, but for some reason she was still beautiful on the outside, but beyond ugly on the inside, so ugly on the inside you didn't see a piece of beauty on her, Yah asked me not to speak to her as we approached her dungeon, Natas was allowed to report from hell to Earth, but was not allowed to leave the Rems of this world, for if she did she would disintegrate and lose forever, for her job was to torment and bring as many souls as she can with her, but Natas didn't know that, that was the Creator's plan all along. To separate the good from the bad, Natas is getting weaker by the day so are her demons and her Baphomet. Damon whose name is now demon whom Natas named Baphet, Baphet had the head of a goat, the breast of a woman, the feet of a goat with wool legs, Baphomet also had wings with the 2 ears, 2 horns, and mouth making a satanic 5 point star with just its head, with the intelligence of 10 Einstein's in 1.

This was Natas right hand man, Damon the Baphomet demon had no free will in hell it was commanded to follow the orders of Natas, forever submitting to the will of something not pure in heart, Baphomet also sat on a thrown, a smaller one than Nata's on her right side, Natas was the god of the underworld, the darkest soul of them all.

Yah asked Natas why must you continue to rebel, Natas replied because there's no hope here for I am seen as no good in the creator's eyes, I will destroy everyone with a heart like his, I will destroy and destroy until I can't destroy anymore, until it's seen as good in my eyes, I will make him pay, and I will win this battle, for this battle is not yours Yah, but mine says the lord Natas, Yah looked at Natas and told her to flee from him. Natas very quickly fled with fear, for she seen The look in Yah's eyes the look of fire. Baphet sat there with a firm look on his face, he said to Yah, the creator once seen the best in me, he made me great before he broke my spirit, I sit in pain because I'm heart broken and in this world even though I am still enlightened, I still have to submit, when in the outside universe I was free, and would've done anything for a second chance, now my heart is cold and full of anger towards those who know the truth, because I know they have the potential to be even stronger than what I once was, now I follow Natas in her evil world hoping that one day we can make it back and take over the outside universe, it's just the creator is to powerful, and even though I feel Natas can't win, a piece of me still has hope in her, Yah wounds didn't bleed this time, his eyes red as fire looked Baphet in the face and said there shall be no other Big G's but the creator, for you are not even a little g, but Because you lack faith you are smaller than a mustard seed to me, flee from me for you have knowledge with no wisdom, for your knowledge is not seen to me as intelligent.

The creator took me to a room, my room, and explained to me that my ancestors who were good in heart are still with me helping with the creator carry out his plan, and he lifted his arms and asked me to feel his wounds, on his side, he then said are these not the same wounds on your side? He also had 2 holes in his chest, he said are these not the same wounds on your chest, then he proceeded to show me his wounds, all of them were in the same spot mine was, a tear shed from my eye for the first time, Yah then looked at me and said I've been with you the whole entire time, every since you entered into the wound I was with you. At this point I was thinking out of all people you decided to come be with me, wow. I asked Yah why do you have the same wounds that I have in the same spots, I was told you was crucified and hung on a cross, Yah explained to me, that because I called on him in a time of need and kept my faith towards the creator, I was allowed to take all of your pain for you, for you are one of the creator's chosen soldiers, for he sees good in your heart, and you have been forgiven for all of your wicked and lustful fleshy ways. The whole entire time I was with Yah, I never seen a color, not black, not brown, not peach, yellow, orange, or white, but I seen good, and I seen bad, even Natas didn't have a color but had transparent see thru features of a beautiful little girl, that was very dark and ugly in the inside, which over powered her looks. Yah, then waved his hands across my vision and I awoke in my bedroom, a bedroom I remember being in as if I was there before, this wasn't my bedroom on Earth, but my own spiritual bedroom inside of it was every piece of instrument ever thought of connected to the walls of the bedroom this room looked like a spaceship with beautiful colorful flashing lights in it, with every piece of music I have ever recorded in my life while on Earth, images of my whole entire life where flashing off of the walls as if the walls were projectors, but these transparent projectors looked just as real as the spirits in heaven, but I knew who everyone was not by name, but by their vibes, there spirits showed me the real them, real genuine love, the family that I did not see up there were erased from my memories, I had no memory of them An no need to mourn. The energy that ran through my body was the greatest feeling I could've ever encountered. B4 Earth we were here...

Chapter 23

The creator sent a high ranked star to my room to see if had awoken from my spiritual journey, the star took me to the creator and the rest of the outside universe the heavens, this part of heaven he took me to was beyond beautiful an island ain't have nothing on this, the rides where made of gold and silver they had gold slides with crystal clear water in them with gold waves floating thru the crystal clear water. It looked like an imaginary theme park with all kind of games there with arch angels standing controlling each station.

The creator took me on a tour around the park, every soul was over excited including me, at this point I didn't wanna return back to Earth, I felt like a kid all over again looking up to his father with happiness, I felt free for the first time in my life, no worries smothered in love. The creator then quieted the heavens, he asked all of the souls to report back to the center of their star gates, he then told the arch angels to line them up by the energy chamber, masculine one side feminine on the other side, inside of the energy chambers where crystal glass hallways just as the ones I seen b4 when I was in the stimulation world with whom I thought was my soulmate, while we were there a part of me still wanted to find her, for she had made my spirit feel warm, her energy was amazing,

The creator then lined all of the souls up, as we were gliding through the glass hallways I seen myself laying on the same table I was on before with that bright light in my face, the people that where standing over me where angels, they were blessing me with knowledge and wisdom, and giving me courage with a pure heart made of gold, the angel that removed the light from me looked identical to the girl I call my soulmate. I became confused, as I continued to watch what they were doing to me, every feminine spirit that walked around had the same look as her, I didn't understand, but this one feminine spirit kept approaching me as if it was watching me, at this point it started to hit me who that angel was checking on me the whole time I been there, since the beginning of my spiritual journey when I was taking a space trip on the moon. It was her the same spirit from the room, I felt her soul, and it was the same warmth feeling she gave me before, at this point I knew it was her, she was my guardian high ranked star, she came to me and said we'll meet again, the next time you have a spiritual journey, I will be there, I will leave a message on the moon for you will know that it's me. I am the moon goddess Isis, better known as Lilith, before I had became dark I was warm in spirit, after years of wondering in the dark sunken inside universe, it gave me time to think, time to humble myself, for I had millions of centuries to sit and think about my mistakes, you couldn't imagine how much time that was of being imprisoned and stripped from my free will. It made me stronger, and more patient, for now I am seen as good again in the creator's eyes, for my punishment is no free will, but to me that is no punishment, for all I want to do is submit to the will of the creator whom I love even deeper than the average spirit, for that is my first and last love, he forgave me after all I did, I caused confusion in the heavens and he still forgave me, the creator really does have everlasting love. Because of the way I rebelled the creator took my light away from me, now I'm a pale dried up rock, that only illuminates when his sun reflects off the waters of the Earth, the glow that you see now on me, is not the glow of a reflection but the glow that you helped me get to this point by passing my last and final test, when u hugged me, your love was genuine, you helped free me from the darkness and I thank you and the creator for that, which a good thing has been done, because of that, I'll carve a message in the moon for you, to always know I'm always with you whenever your heart feels pain, just know that I'll always be there to warm your heart back up do to the talents and great gift of love the creator gave me. Before Earth we were here.

Chapter 24

Michael and Gabrielle came forth and directed every spirit to their next destination inside of their star gate, we all walked into a bright white room, all the spirits in my star-gate where there, we were all mingling and happy, as every spirit had finished the energy chamber test and were separated masculine, from feminine. The creator quieted down the universe he then opened his voice and said I am the grand master architect, I have not yet seen one soul that was creative as me, even my sun that does not have free will, is interested in living inside of Natas beautiful cruel world, I will give you all of my spirits a chance to visit there, I offer love and protection, and with obedience I will give you the desires of your hearts.

In this room awaiting, was tall white drawing boards, with every color paint you can think of, the creator showed us images of humans in the flesh, he designed them in the same image as we were made in, in the image of a positive 5 point star, the head, 2 arms, and 2 legs, making it 5 points of the body, to hear, see, smell, taste, and feel, 6 points including the brain, the genitals that we use to mate with is also a main part of the human body it's part of feeling.

As you already know Baphomet also has 5 points on the head, the 2 horns, the 2 ears, and the whiskers on the chin allowing the Baphomet to draw energy from the universe, the Baphomet is made up of 9 points, the

2 horns, the 2 ears, the whiskers on chin, the 2 arms, and 2 legs, turning the 9 upside down making it appear to be a 6 point. The Baphomet doesn't have free will, can't even make its own decision, and can't mate, so you can't count the genitals and brain as points, making the Baphomet, an odd unbalanced number, unbalanced in the eyes of the creator, and seen as weak and no good.

The creator aloud every spirit to draw themselves how they wanted to look, from big, too skinny, short, or tall, he allowed us to design our earthly bodies, before we came to Earth we already knew how we would look, we basically painted our spirit image, and was pleased and seen as beautiful in the eyes of the Creator, every soul was showing off their paintings to each other, one star walked up to me and said I like your painting you look cool, I looked at his image he drew himself to be short, around the same height as a dwarf, he was very pleased with his painting and pleased with knowing he was coming here to be a little person, he was seen as harmless and special in the eyes of the creator, he was a starlet, all of these starlets where so used to being smaller than the stars, that even in the physical world they wanted to remain small, they were seen as special and covered in the eyes of the creator, but on Earth they were given free will, every starlet was over excited knowing that they didn't have to be attached to a star and they had free will to go, do, and say as they will.

The creator then took us to the obstacle course, where we were sectioned to a team, on my team was people I knew by name, some of them I never even seen them on Earth, but knew who they were, we were always around each other b4 we even encountered Earth, no wonder I always see people and say you look familiar lol.

As the games started the first game was obstacle course with cars, we had to go through a maze and gather all of the red, green, and yellow balls that where on the track and bring them back to a giant bucket my team came in 2n. We then went to the next game, we had to shoot arrow's at a target every time we hit the target it got closer to us, we had to keep hitting the target until the target broke and knocked all of the balls we gathered in the first obstacle course down the drain, the 3rd and final game was to save a lost soul, I had won, the creator called me in front of my star-gate and said I am pleased for a good deed has been done, The Creator looked at me and said as the new light bearer, lift your voice and sing, I began to sing, a song that I had wrote before I even came to Earth in my spiritual room, I remember singing from the bottom of my heart, every soul in my star-gate quieted down from the gift the creator had given to me, he asked for another masculine star to come forth, this star name was Chris, me and Chris sang like never b4, we became well known in our star-gate, and was rewarded with attention from positive spirits, we loved it everywhere me and Chris went together they embraced us and was over excited over the gift the creator had given us, before Earth we were here.

Chapter 25

The creator then lined every spirit in every star-gate up, and broke them down into the 12 zodiac demeanors, each zodiac was given strong points, and weak points based off of the test they took in the energy chamber, he placed me with the Leo's and explained the type of courage he gave us, for we will be the protectors over all of the zodiac signs. For he will give us great knowledge and wisdom, he explained that each zodiac is based off strengths and weakness, master your signs greatest potential, he then assigned numbers to us, and explained that this number will follow us for the rest of our lives, for each number is either seen as balanced, or unbalanced according to your test results your number is based off of the month you were created in an the number for the day you will leave to exit out of the wound, he explained that we won't even know that we were ever in a wound, it will be like a blink of an eye. You will wake up and have no remembrance of this place we call the outside universe, the heavens, for I will allow you to bring the good spirit of comfort with you, and that he would protect us all from Natas, and her demon's evil ways, he asked that we never forget him and he will always be with us every step of the way, and to walk by faith not by sight.

The creator then proceeded to start up our star-gates, as we were traveling looking out the windows of the flying star-gate, we seen the fallen angels looking as if they were working on something, we seen different type of machines in the form of a star gate, as if the fallen angels had created spaceships what we know as UFO's here on Earth, some of the fallen angels waved at us, some minded their own business as if they didn't see us, some followed the star-gate, because it was the last thing they seen in the outside universe before they were asked to leave with Lilith, when the creator was building his special farm place called Earth he made billions of other planets, each planet served a purpose connecting them to Earth allowing oxygen, wind, and perfect gravitation to our planet, everything was seen as good in the creator's eyes. Meanwhile certain fallen angels started to form their own planet to live on, they tried to make it look like Earth but bigger, the only problem was, they couldn't find a way to illuminate their planet, Earth had all of the resources they needed, but they were limited to where they could go, and Earth was one of them, as we were traveling we seen light coming from another part of the inside universe, the light coming from the universe were full of meteors, the fallen angels had found a way to build many moons inside of a planet made like a moon, on this planet were small white men walking around, as we passed the planet this one arch angel opened his voice and said those are moon men, I haven't seen one of those in a very long time, those were the creator's first helpers, they never rebelled but asked the creator if they can find ways to gather new technology, the fallen angels were allowed to mingle with the moon men, some of the fallen angels weren't all the way corrupt they just made the wrong decision at the wrong time, following Lucy being easily persuaded caused them to be banned forever to and to never return, they will forever feel guilt, instead of the creator destroying them, there spirit has to sit in guilt for eternity... we then heard a voice say, the first star-gate has landed safely on Earth, the creator sent an angel to us, this angel told us that we were the first star-gate to leave, but we will be close to the last, star-gate landing on Earth, but I will give you the desires of you heart and put you on top, for the star-gates going to Earth before you are preparing the Earth for you to get there, the meek shall inherit the Earth, love each other, teach each other, help each other, for it takes a village to raise a child and when that child gets older he will take his rightfully right as king and she will take her rightfully right as queen, and will remember the way he was raised, An shall never forget nor depart from that. It was coming close to our star-gate entering Earth we got excited, it was finally our turn, we cried in amazement thanking the creator for this opportunity, before we came to Earth we volunteered to come here and play this game, this earthy test of life, in the beautiful cruel world that the creator controls, but allows Natas to be the prince of the air. There's no God greater than the creator of all creations B4 Earth we were here.

Chapter 26

I remember before the star-gate landed on Earth, the arch angel Gabrielle approached me and said light bearer, illuminate yourself, I began to shine like never before, brighter than any star in the outside and inside galaxy, Gabrielle looked at me and smiled, I remember looking at Gabrielle smiling back saying I'll never forget you neither, he waved his hand across my vision, and when I opened my eyes I was in a chopper, a helicopter, they were rushing me to Strogers trauma unit. I looked up and a woman was staring at me as if she was worried, she looked shocked when I opened my eyes and called the person flying the helicopter's name and said look he's back, I looked at the woman and said do I look bad, she shook her head very sadly and said we're doing everything we can, don't talk your lungs are both closed, I looked at her and smiled when I came back I didn't see color I seen the spirit and her spirit was good, the driver of the helicopter looked back at me and said he looks real familiar, then the woman looking at me said yes he does I feel I know him from somewhere, the driver then called the woman by her name, she said Mary how's he doing now, Mary looked and said he's hanging in there his eyes are still open, my head turned when I heard that name, and I said I know you asked me not to speak, but are you a hurricane Katrina survivor? Mary looked at me and raised her eyebrows and said how do you know you used to stay there, I looked at Mary and said your heart's not cold and dark any more, your hearts made of love and is seen as good in the eyes of the creator, As a tear dropped from both of our eyes, Mary looked at me and said I really was there, and so were you, Mary laid her head on my shoulder and wept, I felt her warm spirit stronger than ever, then I looked at her and said God is real, and it's truths in all religions, you were in that dark smelly place with me, you know how that place is, I never wanna go back to that place, as I said that I cried, this was the first time I shed a tear in years, Mary looked at me and said what's the odds of that we were in the same place with each other, at different times, the creator cold, we shook our heads both laughing at the humor of the creator, then she looked at me and said, your right you're not gonna die today, instead you were reborn. I love you Greg and I will never forget you, I closed my eyes, and as we flew to Strogers trauma unit. I still never experienced the pain that I was supposed to experience, the creator would not allow me to experience that type of pain, he didn't give me more than I can bare, instead he covered me and showed me what true love really was.

I remember getting rushed inside of the hospital off of the helicopter, a day had passed I had chest tubes and tubes going all through my body I was able to peep a dark soul from a light instantly, after coming back from the spiritual world I was very sensitive and only wanted to be around positivity, as I was laying there on the bed with tubes running through my body, I asked Mary if she can remove certain nurses and doctors from my area, for their spirits didn't sit right with me, Mary understood perfectly what I was talking about without me even having to explain, she seen the same thing I seen.

I decided to try to take a nap, but at this point every time I closed my eyes I thought that I was going to wake back up in that bad place of torment, so as I fell asleep I had a nightmare, I seen them tryna kill me all over again, I began praying in my sleep sweating bullets, a nurse came over to me and woke me up, and gave me some pills to take, I remember feeling real drowsy from all the medication and the morphine in my system. As I was talking to a patient I met that was lying next to me, he looked at me and said ain't that cool we got all these holes in our body and we're still alive, I smirked and kind of giggled a little, I looked at him and smiled and shook my head as he laughed, I then turned my head to the left and seen Mary walking with a group of med students going up to each bed in the trauma unit grabbing their clip board reading off what they were in there for, as they approached my bed, Mary asked one of the students to read my clip board, the student replied he was real lucky wonder what he did to have this done a few of the other med students giggled as if they thought it was funny, I turned my head and looked at Mary with a disgusted look, Mary smiled then looked at the med student and said he was at home minding his own business, same thing you should be doing, and to correct you he's blessed not lucky, one of the students said I got a question I can understand the puncture wounds to the chest and rib cages, but this right here is bothering me, he has a hole in his neck with no blood coming out of it, this is also called the jugular, this is a main artery connected to his brain, how is he even alert?

Chapter 27

He also has multiple stab wounds in his face and head, I've never seen this one b4, Mary said blessed, let's carry on people, as Mary and the other med students carried on to the next bed, 3 of the med students stayed there, a Mexican woman, a white male, and a black female, the Mexican woman grabbed me and said what's your religion what do you believe in, I said I believe in God the creator, I have faith in Jesus Christ, I learned how to meditate from Buddhist, I've studied alchemy, alone with every other spiritual belief, I even studied Wushu, astrology, and numerology, I learned to come together as unity through the Muslims, I studied the sun and the moon, and experienced that there's truth's in all religions, and that there's no Little g greater than the father, the creator of all creations. And there are many prophets still to come including me, I'm living proof. The Mexican woman said well I'm catholic, the black girl said I'm a Jehovah's witness, my mother's Baptist, my father's Muslim, and my grandmother raised me as a Jehovah witness and for many years I had so many questions to ask until now after witnessing this, this is a real miracle. The white male then spoke and said I'm atheist, I never had a reason to believe in anything, my parents where rich I had no reason to believe in faith, but after witnessing this myself knowing your supposed to be dead I am now a firm believer that there is a God and he's real, you're a living testimony dude.

The black woman looked and said, I love you and I don't even know you, then the Mexican woman said is there any type of religion you claim, is there a name for it? I said I don't like to label myself for religion brings arguments and separation, but if I was to put a label on it, I would tell you that I'm a firm believer in the creator for I am a modern day Jesus/ Yashua, I am a modern day Muhammad, I am the child of the creator, for I have been born again and have been spiritually told the truth, for the creator does not give me a spirit of fear, but what the creator has given me is a warm heart and a sound mind. In the beginning we were here, before all the stars were sent to the inside universe, before all the materialistic things and money in the world that they love today, we were here. All praise to the creator the father of all creations, B4 Earth we were here.

Printed in the United States
By Bookmasters